D1297606

Science, Religion and Authority: Lessons from the Galileo Affair

The Aquinas Lecture, 1998

SCIENCE, RELIGION AND AUTHORITY: LESSONS FROM THE GALILEO AFFAIR

Under the auspices of the
Wisconsin-Alpha Chapter of Phi Sigma Tau

by

RICHARD J. BLACKWELL

MARQUETTE
UNIVERSITY
PRESS

Library of Congress Cataloging-in-Publication Data

Blackwell, Richard J., 1929-
  Science, religion and authority : lessons from the Galileo affair
/ by Richard J. Blackwell.
    p.   cm. — (The Aquinas lecture; 1998)
  "Under the auspices of the Wisconsin-Alpha Chapter of
Phi Sigma Tau."
  Includes bibliographical references.
  ISBN 0-87462-165-8
  1. Religion and science. 2. Galilei, Galileo, 1564-1642.
3. Bible—Evidences, authority, etc. 4. Bible—Criticism,
interpretation, etc. 5. Church—Authority. I. Title. II. Series.
BL240.2.B62 1998
261.5'5—dc21   97-45287

© 1998 Marquette University Press
Printed in the United States of America

MARQUETTE UNIVERSITY PRESS
MILWAUKEE

The Association of Jesuit University Presse

Prefatory

The Wisconsin-Alpha Chapter of Phi Sigma Tau, the International Honor Society for Philosophy at Marquette University, each year invites a scholar to deliver a lecture in honor of St. Thomas Aquinas.

The 1998 Aquinas Lecture, *Science, Religion and Authority: Lessons from the Galileo Affair,* was delivered in the Todd Wehr Chemistry Building on Sunday, February 22, 1998, by Richard J. Blackwell, Professor of Philosophy at Saint Louis University.

Professor Blackwell received his undergraduate education at the Massachusetts Institute of Technology and at John Carroll University. He earned his Ph.D. in Philosophy at Saint Louis University and then did post-doctoral studies in theoretical physics at John Carroll before returning to Saint Louis University in 1961 where he has taught for the past thirty-seven years. He became Professor of Philosophy in 1966 and held the Danforth Chair in the Humanities from 1986 to 1996.

Professor Blackwell is the author of *Discovery in the Physical Sciences* (1969), *A Bibliography of the Philosophy of Science* (1983), *Christiaan Huygens' "The Pendulum Clock or Geometrical Demonstrations concerning the Motion of Pendula as Applied to Clocks"* (1986), and *Galileo, Bellarmine, and the Bible* (1991). He has translated Thomas Campanella's *A Defense of Galileo, the Mathematician from Florence* (1994), as well as Christian Wolff's *Preliminary Discourse on Philosophy in General* (1963). He translated with others St. Thomas Aquinas's *Commentary on Aristotle's Physics* (1963).

His most recent articles include "Authority in Science and Religion," *Studies in History and Philosophy of Science* (1996), "Methodology in Modern Philosophy," in *Introduction to Modern Philosophy. Contemporary Thinkers: Commentary and Sources* (1995), "Science vs. Religion: Conflict of Ideas or a Clash of Wills?" in *Secularism versus Secularity* (1994), "Foscarini's Defense of Copernicanism," in *Nature and Scientific Method* (1991), "Che cos'e una scoperta scientifica?" *Materiali filosofici* (1984), "Scientific Discovery: The Search for New Categories," *New Ideas in Psychology* (1983), "Reflections on Descartes' Methods of Analysis and Synthesis," in *History of Philosophy in the Making* (1982), "The Rationality of Scientific Discovery," in *Wissenschaftliche und ausserwissenschaftliche Rationalität* (1981), "A New Direction in the Philosophy of Science," *Modern Schoolman* (1981), "In Defense of the Context of Discovery," *Revue internationale de philosophie* (1980), "Descartes' Concept of Matter," in *The Concept of Matter in Modern Philosophy* (1978), and "Science, Objectivity, and Human Values," in *Proceedings of the American Catholic Philosophical Association* (1977).

To Professor Blackwell's distinguished list of publications, Phi Sigma Tau is pleased to add: *Science, Religion and Authority: Lessons from the Galileo Affair.*

For Sarah Elizabeth,
Sarah Jane,
and Thomas John, Jr.

"The crown of the aged is their children's children."
Proverbs 17:6

Contents

Science, Religion and Authority: Lessons from the Galileo Affair

Introduction: An Unstable History

Throughout its long history Christianity has been involved in something like a love-hate relationship with science,[1] or with natural reason as distinct from religious faith, to use the older terminology. There have been times when Christianity has engaged science with great warmth and benefit, usually first in the thinking of an outstandingly creative mind, for example, the synthesis between classical Aristotelian science and Christian theology produced by Thomas Aquinas, who is commemorated in this lecture series. Conversely, science has also benefitted greatly by deriving some of its basic concepts from religious sources. For example, in the seventeenth century the mediaeval conviction that the universe is fundamentally rational gave modern science its initial self-confidence.[2] And the conservation laws in physics, which were introduced at that same time, were originally suggested by the

theological principle of the divine conservation of
the same amount of matter and motion in the universe.[3]

But there have also been other times when science and religion have opposed each other as though
they were two Goliaths at war. The classic example
of this is, of course, Galileo's persistent struggles with
the Catholic Church. Another well-known instance
is the continuing debate over evolution since
Darwin's day.

And at still other times in Western history,
Christianity and science seem to have each gone their
separate ways, sometimes for many generations,
without much explicit conscious concern for the
other's views or well-being. Why is it that the
science-religion relationship has had such an unstable history?

This same question also arises, of course, in the
lived experience of individual men and women. How
should the scientist think and act in an historical
context in which religion predominates, or indeed
even one in which science predominates? Should
this make any difference to the scientist, and why?
Likewise how should the religious believer function
in a world, like ours today, whose culture is dominated by science and technology? In short, how does
the scientist live with religion, and how does the
religious believer live with science? By engaging the
other, by opposing it, or by simply ignoring it?

All of these alternatives have played a role, both
historically and personally, at the interface between
science and religion. And an understanding of them
helps a great deal to appreciate the present state of

the relationship between these two major components of our culture.

Why are tensions between science and religion so persistent? Why do rivalries between science and religion give rise to such strong emotional reactions? Why do such conflicts present at least the appearance, if not the reality, of being irresolvable? These are the questions which we will attempt to answer in this lecture.

We will do this first by looking closely at the Galileo affair to identify the key factors which are relevant to the questions we are asking, and second by formulating a series of lessons from the Galileo affair about the nature of the relationship between science and religion.

Preliminary Historical Considerations: The Strategies of Separation and of Integration

As a preparation for our main argument, we need to say a few things about the general background to the Galileo case. As a first step we might point to the obvious; namely, that both Christianity and science have changed independently of each other over time in response to their own internal requirements and growth. And as a result we find that the science-religion relationship is not one fixed structure but rather has varied considerably over the centuries.

This in turn has led to a great deal of variation in the assessment of science by the Christian community. These reactions have ranged from a rejection of science as dangerous to the goals of religion, to a warm embrace of science as itself a quasi-religious way of finding God, and just about the whole spectrum of attitudes between these extremes. Two of these intermediary views have had special recurring effects up into our own contemporary culture, and are worthy of further consideration, since they help us to understand more clearly the present status of religion in a culture dominated by science and technology. We will call these two views the strategy of separation and the strategy of integration. The former focuses on the differences between science and religion, and attempts, often with a defensive frame of mind, to draw a line of demarcation between the two, so that religion will not become compromised by scientific methods and findings. The latter focuses, usually with a more confident frame of mind, on the similarities between science and religion. Since all truth is consistent in the long run, the objective is to produce an integration of science and religion into one unified cultural whole. Both of these strategies have been successful to some degree, but also both of them have led to problematic consequences which are quite instructive.

For an example of the strategy of separation, let us look at the views of St. Augustine in the early part of the fifth century. He struggled for many years with the question of how the book of Genesis should be interpreted in its literal meaning. He must have felt that the extraordinary creation story with which the Bible opens was heavily challenged by what passed for science in his day, that is, the knowledge of the natural world that had accumulated since the

era of classical Greece. In this very early confrontation between Christianity and science it is clear that
religion was cast in a defensive role, and at times
Augustine seems frustrated. For example, in con-
sidering the scholarly disputes of his day about the
question of the shape of the heavens, he counters
with the following advice:

> Such subjects are of no profit for those who seek
> beatitude, and, what is worse, they take up very
> precious time that ought to be given to what is
> spiritually beneficial. What concern is it of
> mine whether heaven is like a sphere and the
> earth is enclosed by it and suspended in the
> middle of the universe, or whether heaven like
> a disk above the earth covers it over on one
> side?...Hence, I must say briefly that in the
> matter of the shape of the heavens the sacred
> writers knew the truth, but that the Spirit of
> God, who spoke through them, did not wish to
> teach men these facts that would be of no avail
> for their salvation.[4]

This is a very interesting set of remarks. What
is of first importance for religion is, of course, the
spiritual life and the attainment of salvation. Further, the religious life is much more important than
science, which is even described almost as a waste of
time if it is pursued for its own sake, since it makes
no contribution to attaining beatitude. God who is
the author of the Scriptures knows, of course, the
exact structure of the universe, but he has deliber-
ately chosen not to tell us these truths to avoid dis-

tracting us from the real meaning of human life. The purpose of religion is to teach morality and to lead us into the better life which awaits us beyond the grave. Science in contrast is concerned with factual matters in the here and now. Or to make the point in the much later and more famous words of Cardinal Baronius, "The intention of the Holy Spirit is to teach us how one goes to heaven, and not how the heavens go."[5]

If this were all that is involved, then the relationship between science and religion would not be problematic. Each would be a separate realm of human concern which does not impinge upon the other. On this view what is to be recommended in relating science and religion is a strategy of mutual separation. They do not conflict simply because they do not occupy any of the same territory.

But of course this is not all that is involved, as Augustine himself was quite well aware. Both science and religion express views about the structure of the physical world and about some of the events which occur within it. In this area of overlapping claims, science and religion sometimes do not agree. What is one to do then? Again let us listen to Augustine who discusses this situation at some length.

> Usually, even a non-Christian knows something about the earth, the heavens, and the other elements of this world...and this knowledge he holds to as being certain from reason and experience. Now, it is a disgraceful and dangerous thing for an infidel to hear a Christian, presumably giving the meaning of Holy

Scripture, talking nonsense on these topics; and we should take all means to prevent such an embarrassing situation, in which people show up vast ignorance in a Christian and laugh it to scorn. The shame is not so much that an ignorant individual is derided, but that people outside the household of the faith think that our sacred writers hold such opinions, and, to the great loss of those for whose salvation we toil, the writers of our Scripture are criticised and rejected as unlearned men.[6]

Again, in this passage Augustine's pastoral interests are understandably prominent. Non-believers are not at all likely to look with sympathy upon the Christian faith if they are led by incompetent believers to conclude that religious beliefs derived from the Bible are nonsensical. Such non-believers are described as already "certain from reason and experience" about some of their views about the physical world. In short, they have what we would now call scientific convictions which can put the uninformed and overzealous preacher of the Bible to shame. The concern here is to avoid embarrassment and a weakening of the credibility of the Christian message.

Augustine struggled mightily with this issue and ended up with a set of exegetical principles which have defined the science-religion debate ever since.[7] He began with the ancient maxim that all truth is one, since it is all derived from one truthful God. This gives us strong antecedent encouragement to think that ultimately science and religion do not conflict. But this is still too general to guide one any further in a specific dispute, for example, over creationism vs. evolution.

As a next step Augustine accepts the notion, which can be traced back to Aristotle, that natural science can attain absolute truth. This is what he has in mind when he speaks in the passage quoted above about the non-Christian being "certain from reason and experience" concerning some of his views about the natural world. This claim, which is indeed debatable, that full certitude can be established by science as it works from reason and experience is a very important part of our story. We will have frequent occasion to return to this point as we proceed.

At any rate, if this be granted, then it follows that, when a reading of the Bible conflicts with a scientific view which is a certain truth, the Christian must humbly admit that he has interpreted the Scriptures erroneously, and should correct his reading of the Bible to bring it into agreement with such an established scientific truth. This was a wise and considerable qualification introduced by Augustine to reconcile science and the Bible, and has been generally accepted as such ever since.

But what is one to do in the case where a scientific conviction, which is opposed to the Bible, is less than absolutely certain? This is the crux of the matter. Augustine's advice in this case is to give preference to the Bible over science, since the truthfulness of God its author is always stronger than a merely probable judgment based on human reason and sense experience. But granting this, religious views should then be given preference over scientific claims in most cases, since the high standard of absolute proof in science mentioned earlier is so infrequent and so difficult to attain, even in the old view of science before the modern era.

And if it should turn out that scientific laws and theories are never absolutely certain (as most modern commentators on science agree), then biblical views should always be given preference over science. Thus Augustine's principle in this context would result in an hegemony of religion over science in all areas where they overlap. Augustine avoids this consequence only because he accepts the Aristotelian view that demonstrative science can establish absolute truth in at least some cases.

There is also another difficulty which arises from Augustine's principle. For it is also quite possible that what was once a tentative scientific claim could later become fully proven. And thus the Christian believer could be left defending a false idea, if the latter had in the meantime become officially adopted by the Church, the same embarrassing state of affairs which Augustine initially was trying to avoid. And, as we shall see, this is precisely what happened in the Galileo case.

At any rate Augustine's views about evaluating rival claims in science and in the Bible clearly reflect the relative status of natural knowledge and Christianity in the early Church. This relationship had changed dramatically by the early seventeenth century when what we now call modern science made its first appearance in a world heavily influenced by the Renaissance and the Reformation, and hence a world in which religion was much more dominant than science. In contrast to Augustine's defensiveness, we now find some who are much more confident about the interaction between science and religion, and who adopted what we have called the strategy of integration.

Consider, for example, the following remarks by Thomas Campanella, a Dominican philosopher and theologian, who strongly defended Galileo's freedom to pursue his new discoveries in astronomy, even though Campanella personally thought that Galileo had not proven his point, and that he was in fact wrong.

> Anyone who forbids Christians to study philosophy and the sciences also forbids them to be Christians.... Every human society or law which forbids its followers to study the natural world should be held in suspicion of being false. For since one truth does not contradict another,... and since the book of wisdom of God the creator does not contradict the book of wisdom of God the revealer, anyone who fears contradiction by the facts of nature is full of bad faith.[8]

In these remarks there is no concern at all that the pursuit of natural science might interfere with the pursuit of religious salvation. In fact, just the opposite is the case. For Campanella God has chosen to speak to us in two languages: one written in the biblical book of revelation and the other written in the observable book of the physical world. A Christian should read both books to find God wherever He is to be found. Any attempt to block the pursuit of science is, therefore, anti-Christian and anti-religious, for it is an attempt to silence the word of God as spoken in His creation. This is why Campanella so vigorously defended Galileo's freedom of thought. It was not that he was Galileo's friend, or that he even thought that Galileo was right. It was rather the welfare of the Church itself that he was trying to defend. It is very unfortunate that this message was not heard at the time.

We can pursue Campanella's remarks one step further. Since all truth is ultimately one, it should be both possible and desirable to unify science and religion into one unified culture, a goal which Campanella often advocates. This, in effect, is the strategy of integration, just the opposite of the strategy of separation which we mentioned earlier.

Campanella may have been inspired here by the example of his famous Dominican predecessor, who actually succeeded in doing precisely this. I am speaking, of course, of Thomas Aquinas. When the writings of Aristotle finally became fully available in the Latin West in the early thirteenth century, they were rightly seen as anti-Christian, and as a result they were not allowed to be taught in the classrooms at that time. The main complaints were that Aristotle had maintained that the world is eternal, that the human soul is not immortal, and that God has no providential concern at all for humans and the material world in general. These Aristotelian teachings cut at the heart of the religious world view. One cannot consistently be both a strict Aristotelian and a Christian, as Campanella constantly reminds us.

Nevertheless Aquinas undertook as his lifework the seemingly impossible task of reconciling Aristotelian philosophy and science with the Catholic faith. And he succeeded in doing this by reconceptualizing some of the key ideas in Aristotle and in what was traditional Christian theology up to that time. Because of this reconceptualization, his undertaking was a risky business. For in addition to redefining some concepts from Aristotle, some older patterns of theological thinking also had to be modified. And in both cases Aquinas needed to provide independent empirical evidence, rational argumentation, and textual support to avoid the criticism that his synthesis of the two was merely a "Rube Goldberg" contrivance.

As we said, this was risky business. Two years after Aquinas' death a number of his teachings were condemned by the Bishop of Paris. Yet in time the Thomistic synthesis became accepted as the new orthodoxy. And by now we might tend to forget that Thomism was not originally given to the Apostles, but was generated considerably later by a creative rethinking of both an anti-Christian Aristotle and the theology of that day. Campanella never tires of reminding us that such an enterprise is an important responsibility of the Christian philosopher and theologian.

If Campanella is right, then one wonders whether another such integration could happen again today between religion and modern science. The prospects for that happening however are minimal, because the strategy of integration always involves the need to reconceptualize some components of the two disciplines being merged. But this process of reconceptualization is understandably then always upsetting to the religious community as found in its institutional church, precisely because the latter has the custodial role of conserving and protecting the original revelation intact. A recent case of this is the controversy initiated by Teilhard de Chardin's attempt to reconceptualize the Christian revelation on the basis of an evolutionary metaphysics. So, like the strategy of separation, the route of integration entails problematic consequences, which in turn are instructive as to why the science-religion relationship is so fragile and unstable.

At any rate the views of Augustine and of Aquinas are still important influences on how we think today about the relationship between science and religion. However, these views have been filtered down to us through the Galileo affair, which has changed the picture drastically. The fact that this episode is still studied and referred to so widely, that it is represented and misrepresented so often in our day, shows that it is the central factor in shaping the attitude of the modern mind on the more general question of the relations between science and religion.

A Brief Sketch of the Galileo Affair

Despite the numerous controversies of interpretation which swirl around the Galileo affair, the basic facts of the case are now quite well known. Furthermore a delineation of these facts reveals the key parameters which have characterized the relationship between science and religion ever since. This at least allows us to identify the factors which define the science-religion dispute, which is our main concern, without becoming bogged down in evaluating the many controversies of the partisans on both sides.

With this in mind we will now first give an historical sketch of what happened in the Galileo affair, and then list five lessons to be learned from it. One of the basic facts about the Galileo affair, which has considerable consequences for our interests in this lecture, is that it consisted of two trials, not just one. The first trial took place in February of 1616; the second trial seventeen years later in the spring of 1633. The first trial made a judgment about a question of truth; the second about a question of legal culpability. The first trial dealt with matters of fact; the second with matters of authority. The first trial occurred at an abstract level; the second at a personal level. Let us see whether we can explain this more concretely.

We know from his personal correspondence[9] that at least by 1597 Galileo had become personally convinced that the sun is located in the center of the world, and that the earth and the other planets revolve around the sun in orbits having regular periods. This was an old theory, first entertained by some of the ancient Greek astronomers, and then reintroduced[10] by Copernicus in 1543. In the period between Copernicus and Galileo it remained just that, a theory, which the professional astronomers debated warmly among themselves, but which did not have much of a wider influence.

The turning point came in 1610 by which time Galileo had constructed his telescope, which he then turned for the first time to the observation of the heavens.[11] He made a host of new discoveries of great importance; for example, the mountains and valleys on the moon, four of the moons of Jupiter, the rings of Saturn (although he did not realize what they were), sunspots, and of special importance, the phases of Venus. He began to publish these observations, along with his interpretations of them, and in the process the heliocentric theory was transformed from a curious speculation among astronomers to a view of the world which seemed, even to the generally informed reader, to be more and more probably the true description of the solar system.

In these early writings Galileo's previous convictions about heliocentrism gradually became more explicit. But it is very important to emphasize that he did not have a strict proof. The closest he came at that time was the evidence that Venus goes through a full set of phases, as does our own moon. This proves that Venus (and probably Mercury also) revolves around the sun, but it does not determine whether the earth also revolves around the sun, rather than vice versa. Galileo was quite well aware that he did not have a conclusive proof of this point, as is evident from the fact that for the rest of his life he kept up his search for the conclusive proof. But all of his efforts in this direction failed him, including his famous claim that the ocean tides are caused by the double motion of the earth required by Copernicus' theory. Galileo's work on these questions were methodologically routine scientific inquiries in which theories are proposed and tested against the authority of empirical facts and their rational interpretation.

But another type of authority soon entered into the picture. There are many apparently conflicting passages in the Bible which state either directly or by implication that the earth is at rest in the center of the universe, and that the sun revolves around the earth from east to west. That is not surprising, since still today common sense clearly indicates that Copernicanism is wrong on this point. Galileo's opponents were quick to point out this apparent inconsistency between the new astronomy and the Scriptures. The best known of these passages[12] is, of course, Joshua's petition to God to stop the sun in its tracks so that Joshua's army could continue and win its battle at Gibeon.[13] Another frequently cited passage was the description of the sun in Psalm 19: 4-6:

> High above, he pitched a tent for the sun,
> who comes out of his pavilion like a bridegroom,
> exulting like a hero to run his race.
> He has his rising on the edge of the heaven,
> the end of his course is its furthest edge,
> and nothing can escape his heat.

In short, the new astronomy seemed to say, in effect, that the Bible is in error when it speaks about the motion of the sun and the immobility of the earth.

Any attempt to deal with this issue in the Catholic parts of Europe was made doubly difficult because of the Reformation, the subsequent Counter Reformation, and the atmosphere leading to the religious wars which were about to begin. As a result the Catholic Church at that time was especially sensitive not only about questions of reinterpreting Scripture, but also about the issue of who properly possessed the authority to undertake such interpretations, which had been a debate of major importance during the Reformation. This authority was explicitly located by the Catholic Church in the hands of the bishops by an important decree issued at the Fourth Session of the Council of Trent (8 April 1546). The relevant passage reads as follows.

> Furthermore, to control petulant spirits, the Council decrees that, in matters of faith and morals pertaining to the edification of Christian doctrine, no one, relying on his own judgment and distorting the Sacred Scriptures according to his own conceptions, shall dare to interpret them contrary to that sense which Holy Mother Church, to whom it belongs to judge of their true sense and meaning, has held and does hold, or even contrary to the unanimous agreement of the Fathers, even though such interpretations should never at any time be published. Those who do otherwise shall be identified by the ordinaries and punished in accordance with the penalties prescribed by the law.[14]

Although this decree was issued eighteen years before Galileo was born, he and his friends may well have had a feeling that it was somehow written with Galileo already in mind as one of the "petulant spirits." At any rate the confrontation between Copernicanism and the Bible occurred subsequently at two levels: (1) how should the relevant passages in the Bible be interpreted on this issue? and, (2) as is directly addressed in the decree from Trent, who had the authority to undertake such an interpretation, or better, reinterpretation?

Galileo, of course, not being a bishop and having no training in theology, was in no position to enter the scriptural debate, and he knew that he could never possibly win on that battlefield. But he did the next best thing. He was bold enough to write a short pamphlet, in the form of a *Letter to the Grand Duchess Christina* (1615), in which he examined the general principles of biblical exegesis that would apply to the coming debate regarding scripture and science.[15]

He based his analysis heavily on the views of St. Augustine concerning the levels of meaning and of interpretation of the Bible. For example, in the case of a conflict, if science has succeeded in conclusively proving a claim about the world, then Scripture should be interpreted accordingly. On the other hand, if we know that it is impossible for science to prove a claim about the world, then Galileo concedes that preference should be given to the Bible, although he does not tell us how we would establish such an impossibility. This still leaves a very large middle ground unaccounted for, namely, what science could prove, but has not done so to date. And unfortunately the Copernican theory falls into this middle ground.

Perhaps Galileo intended one to conclude that in such cases the recommended course of action is to leave the matter open for the time being. As the saying puts it, "When in doubt, do nothing." The closest that Galileo came to this is his reminder that many biblical passages are open to multiple interpretations, and in such cases it is best not to fix the meaning of Scripture one way or the other, lest later proof contradict the option taken. This is prudent advice. And in effect this was precisely the course taken by the Church in another theological debate of that era between the Jesuits and the Dominicans over the reconciliation of human free will and divine knowledge and power.[16] If Galileo's similar advice had been taken on the Copernican question, it would have at least temporarily postponed the conflict that was gathering steam.

Galileo also made extensive use of the distinction between literal and metaphorical uses of language in the Bible, which had long been standard among exegetes, and of the related principle that the Scriptures are accommodated to the understanding of the common person. To the modern mind, this is the level at which the problem should have been resolved. To the argument based on the decree of Trent, that one must accept the common agreement of the Fathers of the Church on interpreting Scripture, Galileo perceptively replied that there was no agreement among the Fathers on heliocentrism since they never had any occasion to be concerned about the matter in their day, and thus they merely used the language of uncritical common sense when they say that the sun rises and sets. Much more substantially, the decree of Trent had required the acceptance of the Church's reading of Scripture with the explicit limitation to "matters of faith and morals." Galileo gingerly raised the question of whether the structure of the heavens is indeed a "matter of faith and morals." As we shall see, Cardinal Bellarmine later focused the dispute on this point.

At any rate Galileo's engagement of the issues at the level of the principles of exegesis was masterfully executed. His *Letter to the Grand Duchess Christina* has since become a minor classic in the field of biblical interpretation, even though, ironically enough, it was written by a scientist with no training in theology.

At this point matters became considerably more complicated by the unanticipated actions of a Carmelite theologian Paolo Antonio Foscarini, who published a small book entitled *Letter on the Motion of the Earth.*[17] Foscarini did not know Galileo personally, but was sympathetic toward his scientific work. He understood that the new astronomy had not yet been conclusively proven. But using Augustine's maxim, he argued that, since it may well be proven in the near future, the Church would at that time need to reinterpret the biblical passages that appear to say the opposite. His book was devoted to providing these reinterpretations in considerable detail ahead of time, as a service to the future requirements of the Church.

Furthermore Foscarini sent a copy of his treatise to Cardinal Bellarmine for his assessment, an action which may well have made a public decision on the matter by the Church inevitable. Bellarmine replied in a letter to Foscarini, which succinctly stated the Church's position under three headings.[18]

First, no problems arise at all when astronomers use the Copernican theory "hypothetically," that is, as a means of making calculations and predictions concerning the motions of the heavens. He added gratuitously that he had always thought that both Copernicus and Galileo wrote only hypothetically. But if one takes this theory realistically, that is, as an account of how the heavens are actually structured and moved, then that is "dangerous," to use Bellarmine's own word, since that undermines the faith and the authority of the Scriptures.

Second, those who would say that the motion of the sun and the immobility of the earth are not "matters of faith and morals," as mentioned in the decree of the Fourth Session of the Council of Trent, are in error. For this is included in the faith, not because of the subject matter involved, but simply because that is what is said in the Bible, all of whose statements must be true because of its divine authorship. When pushed to its full consequences, this makes the Bible out to be, among other things, a textbook about the physical world to be accepted in all cases where science has not strictly proven a conflicting claim. In our judgment Bellarmine's view on this point effectively and authoritatively ended discussion of the issue, since it gave Galileo and his friends no further room to maneuver.[19]

Third, using Augustine's maxim, Bellarmine concedes that if and when the Copernican theory ever were to be proven, the Church would need either to reinterpret the contrary biblical passages, or at least to say that we do not understand them. But no such proof has been produced to date, and there is great doubt in Bellarmine's mind that it can be produced.

And thus the matter was formulated by Bellarmine, who was the papal theologian at this critical time.

As a result of these and other events, a public statement about the Copernican issue was in order. In February of 1616, the Congregation of the Holy Office decided that Copernican astronomy was false because it is contrary to the Scriptures. Pope Paul V accepted this recommendation of the Holy Office, and a decree of the Congregation of the Index was published on 5 March 1616, which publicly announced the decision. The relevant passage of that decree reads as follows.

> It has come to the attention of this Sacred Congregation that the Pythagorean doctrine of the mobility of the earth and the immobility of the sun, which is false and completely contrary to the divine Scriptures,...is now being divulged and accepted by many...Therefore, lest this opinion spread further and endanger Catholic truth, it is ordered that Nicholas Copernicus' *De revolutionibus orbium*...be suspended until corrected;[20] also that the book of the Carmelite Father Paolo Antonio Foscarini is completely

prohibited and condemned; and also that all
other books teaching the same thing are prohibited, as the present Decree prohibits, condemns,
and suspends them all respectively.[21]

This decree was the final judgment in the first
Galileo trial. It was based on a serious theological
error, as the present Pope John Paul II has recently
gone out of his way to state: "The error of the theo-
logians of the time when they maintained the cen-
trality of the earth was to think that our understanding of the physical world's structure was in some
way imposed by the literal sense of Sacred Scripture."[22] As we read the documents, this error was
grounded primarily in Bellarmine's broad interpretation of the phrase "matters of faith and morals" as
used in the decree of the Council of Trent. To put it
in philosophical terms, to decide a scientific question by the use of a religious authority is to commit
a category mistake. But however it be accounted for,
the damage was done.

But the matter did not end here. It is important to note that neither Galileo's name, nor any of
his writings, were mentioned in the decree of con-
demnation. He, of course, knew that he would have
been bound by that decree, like any other member
of the Church. But Pope Paul V did not think that
that was enough. He instructed Bellarmine to meet
with Galileo and to observe the following three-point
agenda at their meeting: (1) to inform Galileo of
the decision to condemn Copernicanism and to ask
for his acceptance of that decision; (2) if Galileo
were to refuse, to impose on him an injunction to

abstain from advocating Copernicanism; and (3) if he should still not agree, Galileo was to be imprisoned. The severity of these instructions, to the extent of even anticipating possible imprisonment, indicates a very great concern in Paul V's mind over the control of Copernicanism.

The meeting took place one week before the decree was issued. Exactly what happened at that meeting is, very unfortunately, not clear. For there are two accounts of it which survive, but they are inconsistent.

The record of the meeting on file at the Holy Office says that Galileo was placed under an injunction, specifically that he should not "hold, teach, or defend it [Copernicanism] in any way, either verbally or in writing." But Galileo had the presence of mind to ask Bellarmine, three months after the meeting, for a letter summarizing what had transpired to protect his own reputation and future interests in the matter. Bellarmine's letter says that the only thing that happened was that Galileo was informed of the pending decree condemning Copernicanism, with the result that it "cannot be defended or held."[23] No mention was made by Bellarmine of any injunction being imposed on Galileo. Galileo, of course, never saw the document in the files of the Holy Office, and the Holy Office in turn did not know about Bellarmine's letter to Galileo. In many ways one of the most extraordinary parts of the whole story is the confusion over what happened at the Galileo-Bellarmine meeting, and the disastrous consequences that this would cause later. To this day it is still not known exactly what happened.

For the next seventeen years Galileo stayed out of harm's way simply by working on other scientific problems, and by not publishing anything further on Copernicanism. He did however begin quietly to write a new book on the old dispute.

The reason for this is that his good friend and fellow Tuscan, Cardinal Maffeo Barberini, had been elected Pope Urban VIII in 1623. The new Pope was a man of high cultural interests and accomplishments of his own. He met with Galileo on several occasions about the status of the new astronomy. As before, hypothetical discussion of Copernicanism was not seen as a problem. So Galileo decided, apparently with the impression that he had at least the tacit approval of the Pope, to write a detailed analysis of all the evidence and arguments in favor of, and in opposition to, both the old geocentric and the new heliocentric world views. Further he cast the book in the literary form of a dialogue, thus claiming to present defenders of both views in a neutral way. This book, entitled *Dialogue Concerning the Two Chief World Systems,* has become a classic in Italian literature. But quite ironically Galileo's old friend, Pope Urban VIII, was destined later to condemn it.

Galileo's book created a sensation when it appeared early in the year 1632. One of the reasons was that it was rather clear to all who read it that the dialogue strongly favored Galileo's spokesman, who presents and defends the Copernican point of view. It thus seemed to be a direct violation of the decree of 1616. To make matters much worse, the record of the Bellarmine-Galileo meeting in 1616

was found in the files of the Holy Office. Thus
Galileo was also open to the charge that he had vio-
lated the injunction reported in that document,
which had stated that he was not to advocate Copernicanism "in any way, verbally or in writing," a
blanket prohibition which certainly would have cov-
ered the *Dialogue*.

It turned out that this was the first time that
Urban VIII became aware of the injunction, and he
was furious with Galileo for not mentioning that at
their meetings a few years earlier. Galileo in turn
maintained later at the trial that he had always been
guided by the terms in his letter from Bellarmine,
which does not mention any injunction, and that
he had not remembered the putative injunction.

At any rate a trial became inevitable on these
charges, and it took place in Rome in the spring of
1633. In studying the transcripts[24] of the trial, one
cannot help noticing something special. There are
no assessments of, or interrogations about, the evidence and arguments regarding Copernicanism, no
use of biblical quotations to the contrary, no discussion of the principles of scriptural exegesis, no
analysis of the standards of scientific proof. All of
these issues relate to deciding the factual question
of the structure of the heavens, and that issue had
been fully settled in 1616 as far as the Church was
concerned.

So Galileo's second trial was not in any real sense
a direct assessment of science vs. religion. Rather it
was a personal judgment about Galileo's loyalty and
obedience to the requirements laid down in the de-

cree and the injunction of 1616. The interrogations focused almost completely on these matters, and on the related problem of how Galileo had managed to get the needed ecclesiastical permissions to publish his book. The court's concern was his personal culpability in these areas, especially regarding the injunction. The trial was not about truth in science, but about authority in the Church.

The dramatic high point of the trial occurred when Galileo presented a copy of his letter from Bellarmine giving the sense of their meeting in 1616. The judges were looking, however, at a different account in the Holy Office's report which they held in their hands. Unfortunately Cardinal Bellarmine had died twelve years earlier. A personal word from him would have been enough to settle the case, and perhaps in Galileo's favor, judging from his letter. But as we all know, the court decided against Galileo.

The relevant part of the court's judgment reads as follows:

> We say, pronounce, sentence, and declare that you, the above-mentioned Galileo, because of the things deduced in the trial and confessed by you as above, have rendered yourself according to this Holy Office vehemently suspected of heresy, namely, of having held and believed a doctrine which is false and contrary to the divine and Holy Scripture,...and that one may hold and defend as probable an opinion after it has been declared and defined [to be] contrary to the Holy Scripture.[25]

Note that this was not a judgment that Copernicanism is false and contrary to the Scriptures. That
decision had already been made at the first Galileo
trial seventeen years earlier. Rather it was a judgment against Galileo personally for violating the
decree and the injunction.

The destructive impact of these events has, of
course, been enormous, and it continues today. The
myths that have grown up around the Galileo affair
are, indeed, legendary. Probably nothing else has had
a stronger influence in bringing about the contemporary view that the relationship between science
and religion is a contentious one. But there is also a
positive side to this story. For study of this episode
helps to delineate rather precisely the differences between science and religion, and how they interact
with each other. It is to this topic that we now turn
our attention in the form of five lessons to be learned
from the Galileo affair.

Lessons from the Galileo Affair

*1. There is a fundamental difference between a
description of the way things are, and a justification of
a description which authorizes its truth.* This is best
seen simply by looking at a few examples.

If we are told that the bombing of Pearl Harbor
took place on a Sunday, we know what that means.
Whether that is also true is another question. And
we can authorize that claim to be true in a variety of
ways; for example, testimony from eyewitnesses,
contemporary newspaper accounts, history books,
military records.

After Copernicus had said that the planets revolve around the sun which is fixed at the center of
the universe, both sides in the ensuing dispute understood what that meant. The argument was over
whether that description of things was true, and especially over what should count as a method of au-
thorizing its truth or establishing its falsity. Today
physicists would agree with Galileo on the nature
of the authority behind the truths of science. But
they would also say that both his description of the
world system and its earlier geocentric rival are actually wrong, since there is no center to the universe. And as an important recent study has shown,[26]
Cardinal Bellarmine personally also thought that
both of the rival astronomical theories of his day
were wrong. But his reason was that the authority
behind the account in Genesis reveals a very different model of the universe, and that view should be
preferred as true because it is based on a higher type
of authority. As these comparisons show, the descriptive and authority levels interact in complex ways,
producing differing results for differing reasons.

Another example: when Galileo claimed that
the sun rotates on its own axis once in approximately
twenty-eight days, that at the time was a quite new
description of the way things are. His authority for
saying this was located in a complex combination
of new data about sunspots, precise measurements
of their motions, and critical analysis of all this in-
formation; in short, in an appeal to sensory evidence
and its rational interpretation.

When Christianity speaks about the creation of
the world, or about a life after death, these are also

descriptions of what is said to be the way things are. The authorization of the truth of these claims, however, is obviously not located in sensory fact and rational interpretation, as in the sciences, but in a religious tradition which is ultimately traced back to what is revealed in the Scriptures understood to be the word of God.

Again, as we have seen earlier, Galileo's first trial revolved around a dispute located primarily at the descriptive level. His second trial dealt almost exclusively with issues located at the authority level. And these two levels interacted in very complex ways throughout the Galileo affair, as we have already seen in some detail.

The point of all these examples is simply to illustrate the distinction between description and authorization. This is not to deny that at both of these levels one may find considerable difficulty in being specific. Thus it is not easy to determine precisely what is meant by the descriptive terms which refer to the world system, or sunspots, or creation, or an afterlife. Also there are complex debates over what authorizes scientific truth and what authorizes religious beliefs.

All that we are saying for now is that the descriptive level is distinct from the authority level in human knowledge, and that, as the above examples show, both of these levels are found in our everyday knowledge, in science, and in religion. If this be granted, then it follows that science and religion interact with each other at both of these levels.

2. Science and religion sometimes agree, sometimes disagree, at the descriptive level, but they are always different from each other at the level of authority. Most scientific descriptions have no counterpart in religion. And most religious descriptions have no counterpart in science. But there is also an area of overlap where the two sets of descriptions refer to the same subject matter, and in that area they may either agree or disagree in what is claimed.

When they agree, the historical tendency has been to praise the unity of truth, which is frequently accounted for by the notion that all truth comes from one source, namely, God as the author of both the book of revelation and the book of nature, to use the phrase so popular in Galileo's day. But it should be noted that such agreement at the level of description does not erase the basic difference between science and religion at the level of authority. Science retains its epistemic authority of appealing to sensory evidence and rational interpretation. And religion retains its epistemic authority of appealing to religious tradition and revelation in Scripture as its standard of truth. These differences are always present; otherwise science would no longer be science, and religion would no longer be religion.

On the other hand, when they disagree, the historical tendency has been the generation of antagonisms between science and religion, which have been unusually sharp and long-lasting. Why is that the case? The answer to this question is located at the level of the respective authorities behind science and religion. The disagreements arise first and explicitly at the descriptive level, but they soon cut through to the more fundamental level of authority, as is evident in the Galileo case, whether the combatants are aware of it or not. Why does this happen? This brings us to our central point.

3. At the authority level neither science nor religion are purely rational in character. Each involves a volitional component derived from the human will, albeit in very different ways. This volitional factor is the main reason why disagreements between science and religion so easily become antagonistic and emotional. Since this point is, as we said, central to our argument, it needs to be justified in some detail by comparing the characteristics of religious and scientific authority.

The easier case to grasp is what happens in science, partly because scientists and philosophers of science in the twentieth century have subjected scientific method to a detailed analysis, which has by now become widely accepted. The main factors in this account which are germane to our considerations are the following.

First, empirical laws are formulated in science by the process of inductive generalization, which has been recognized from at least the time of Aristotle as not being logically sound. Simply put, if something is true of part of a class, it does not follow from that fact that it is also true of the class as a whole. It could be true of the whole class, of course; but also the next case could be a negative instance. So even if we have an exceptionless body of data, the generalized conclusion is still only highly probable. Innumerable attempts throughout the history of science to resolve this problem of conclusively justifying universal claims by means of enumerative induction have met with failure.

Second, science uses a process of reasoning called abduction, or retroduction, which generates theoretical hypotheses about non-observables, which hypotheses are used to explain empirical laws and data. That this occurs in science is clear. But how such abductive inferences are made, and in what sense they are rationally justified, is not at all clear.[27]

Third, general laws and explanatory theories, once generated, are then put to an empirical test in the process of verification. This also is not logically sound. For if the consequences of an hypothesis are true, it does not follow logically that the hypothesis itself is true. The results could be due to some other hypothesis or cause.

Nevertheless, despite these deficiencies, scientists use inductive, abductive, and verificational methods regularly in the hope and faith that they will obtain correct results more often than not. In an attempt to avoid these logical problems, Karl Popper[28] developed a popular model of science, in which induction and verification play no role, but which is based instead on the process of falsification, which is logically valid. But ultimately even he had to conclude that the original genesis of scientific hypotheses is a non-rational process, and that we can only prove that hypotheses are false, but never that they are true. As is evident from all this, the rules by which science operates are not fully rational in the sense of not being fully logical, yet the scientist chooses to proceed using such rules.

Fourth, after the influential work of Thomas Kuhn[29] in the 1960's, it is now widely agreed that the normal life of science occurs within an unexamined set of background assumptions about the world and our ability to know it. These paradigms, as Kuhn calls them, are uncritically accepted by normal science, and come under direct attention only when science is in a state of revolutionary crisis caused by internal anomalies. Even then two or more rival paradigms cannot be directly compared or mutually evaluated without committing category mistakes, because for Kuhn there is no such thing as a theory-neutral stance. In short, paradigms are incommensurable to some degree, and hence the choice of one paradigm over another injects once again a non-rational factor into science. This is the main message from Kuhn's now famous account of how science grows and changes over time.

The net result of all this is that we find built into science at the level of its epistemic authority a series of choices to adopt certain rules of procedure, namely, induction, abduction, verification and paradigm commitments, which are not themselves fully justifiable on rational grounds. These rule choices contain an element of volition, that is, a contribution from the human will. These choices are made because trial and error have shown these rules to have been practically successful in the past, and in the hope that they will continue to succeed in the future. If and when these choices and hopes become challenged by another type of authority, as happened in the Galileo case, the scientific community can be expected to become upset, to oppose the challenge, and not to forget it.

On the other hand something analogous to this happens in religion, which also contains a voluntary component, although it functions in a quite different way. This is not a new idea. It has had a long history in traditional theology as found in the explication of the nature of the personal act of religious belief. In short, religious faith has traditionally been understood to be primarily an act of knowledge. One knows that something is true. But the distinctive characteristic of an act of religious faith is that the motive for assenting to something as true, for example, that there is a life after death, is not direct factual evidence or rational proof. Rather it is the believer's willingness to accept the authority of a witness. To use the old terminology, an act of faith is an act of the intellect whose assent is determined by an act of the will.[30]

This may sound somewhat mysterious, but it is really quite straightforward. For most of our natural, common sense, *non-religious* beliefs have the same characteristics. For example, if I tell you that I have two sons, you now know something that you may not have known before from direct acquaintance with my family. You have acquired a new piece of knowledge. Why do you assent to that as true? Simply because you believe me, you trust me, you are willing to accept my word on this point as reliable. Of course, I may intend to mislead you, or in my old age I may have forgotten how many sons I have, or you may have misunderstood my remarks. There is no guarantee of incorrigible truth here, but the fact is that a very large part of our true natural knowledge is acquired in this way. The important point for our concerns is that such routine natural beliefs are based in part on an act of the will, that is, on a choice to accept the word of a witness as reliable.

The same is true of a religious belief, for example, that there is a life after death. If one believes this, one claims to know something, and not just to hope something, about the future. But the motive for assent is certainly not direct, factual experience. It is rather the acceptance of the authority of the word of others in the religious tradition, which in turn traces back ultimately to the revelation reported in the Scriptures. In the classical view, of course, God is the original authority behind the revelation. How that affects the truth value of religious claims is a very complex question, but fortunately that is not our concern here. Our point simply is that religious belief involves an act of choice at its very core, that is, as its motive for assent. For science, on the other hand, the motive for assent is empirical fact and rational proof, which nevertheless also involve different kinds of choices, as we have seen.

In summary, if this analysis is correct, then at the level of their authority both science and religion involve not only rational understanding but also complex volitional commitments, albeit in different ways. These voluntary aspects of science and religion become most prominent when they come into conflict. This is especially true when religion is challenged by science, because the volitional factor is located at a much more fundamental level in religion than it is in science. Thus the authority of religion is more easily threatened, as is evident in the Galileo case.

The human will is involved in religion in another quite different way which is also germane to our main theme. As we have seen, religious faith consists of a set of knowledge claims which are taken on authority by the believer to be true about God, the world, and the human person. However, the acquisition and contemplation of this fund of knowledge is not what religion is all about, nor is this even the primary purpose of religion. The main point rather is for the religious believer to make a personal commitment to live his or her life according to the norms and guidelines of the religious message, and to carry out that commitment. It is not just truth, but moral good and salvation, which is the goal. It is not abstract knowledge, but concrete human action in the real world, which is the focus of religion. Religion does not just appeal to reason; it also makes demands on the will regarding one's personal life.

Now in order to make the move from contemplated understanding to committed action in the world, the religious believer must make a volitional choice to act out the religious life style described in the faith. In short, the religious person commits himself or herself to a life guided by faith. Such a self-commitment is a very heavy investment on the part of the believer. As a result much more than merely an abstract debate is at issue if, at some later time, that self-commitment is threatened because science seems to indicate that it is based on one or more false beliefs.

In science this type of self-commitment does
not operate, or at least it is not present in the same
sense as in religion. There are, of course, many very
highly committed scientists. But this usually, if not
always, refers to their firm allegiance to the value of
doing science, and to the value of the truths it es-
tablishes, perhaps even for some to the point of a
sort of fanaticism akin to religious fanaticism. But
such self-commitment to science is not, at least in
any usual sense, a commitment to a specific
day-to-day life style or value system *dictated by the
content of science itself.* But we need not tarry on this
point. If the listener is persuaded that the same type
of personal self-commitment found in religion is also
found in science, then that would make our case
even stronger; namely, that neither science nor religion are purely rational enterprises, since they also
contain elements of human choice.

4. *Tensions at the authority level have become
amplified as science and religion have gradually become institutionalized over a long period of time.*

As we have already seen, Galileo's notion that
science is based on the authority of evidence and its
rational interpretation remains in place, although
even now scientists and philosophers of science still
do not agree on precisely how that happens. Mean-
while that authority has become institutionalized
along lines which are almost universally accepted
today.

Both experimental claims and explanatory hypotheses in science must be submitted to multiple,
public testings. No individual scientist embodies the

full authority of science. The whole process is governed by the methods of public verification and falsification, and thus is self-corrective in character because of the feedback effect of falsification. Across the board the conclusions that survive this process of scientific investigation are understood to be fallible, no matter how strong the evidence for them may be.

As a result the authority behind science, which was originally championed by Galileo, has come in time to be exercised and institutionalized in the scientific community as pluralistic, public, fallibilistic, and self-corrective.

On the other hand exactly the opposite characteristics can be seen to be present in Galileo's day in biblically based religion. And these characteristics have become even more pronounced since then in the Church which challenged Galileo. That authority consists fundamentally in the power of the spoken and written word of revelation, and thereby in the credibility of the author of that message.

Partly because of the Catholic Church's origins in the era of the Roman Empire, its authority became institutionalized into a highly centralized and imperial ecclesiastical structure, which was created to serve as the custodian of the spoken and written word of God. Indeed the very word "authority" originally referred to the divine "author" to whom one appeals to justify a belief in the religious revelation. As the centuries passed, that authority became more and more concentrated in the hands of a few church leaders at the episcopal level, who thought alike, who tended to make decisions in private, and whose weight of office as custodians of the revelation made them quite self-protective and resistant to change.

To put this in another way, since the institutional authority of the Church is grounded in the epistemic authority of Scripture and tradition, then whatever threatens, or is perceived to threaten, the former is also seen as a threat to the latter. This is what happened in the Reformation, and shortly afterwards in the Galileo affair, which may well have been perceived by some Church officials at that time as the second wave of the Reformation. At any rate the integrity and welfare of the Church as an institution tended to become a primary concern, since it had come to embody the authority on which the entire religious culture was based.

This centralizing tendency can easily be seen over the centuries in the increasing appeals to tradition and the early Church Fathers, in the conciliar movement in the Church, in the increasing authority of the Popes, in the clash with the reformers over the individual vs. the hierarchy as the locus for the interpretation of the Bible, and more recently in the teaching of papal infallibility.

Consequently the authority behind scripturally based religion, at least in the Catholic tradition, became monolithic, centralized, esoteric, resistant to change, and self-protective.

As a result of all this, it should be much clearer to us today than it could ever have been to Galileo himself, for whom the new science was not yet fully understood, that the institutionalized authorities behind science and behind scripturally based religion have very different, indeed to some degree even opposed, characteristics. Each is intended to provide justification for the claims which it proposes. But that justification process engenders a mind-set which is quite different in the two cases. Those who are well trained in either often find it very difficult to comprehend the mode of thinking employed in the other. Even our present systems of higher education sometimes seem designed to amplify, and not to mediate, these differences.

Of course, there is always the option of simply denying that any authority resides in religion, or in science, thereby resolving the issue by simply rejecting its existence. And one could no doubt find some who defend either of these alternatives. But doing this will not make either religion or science disappear. The question of the legitimacy of their authorities will remain.

At any rate Galileo's relocation of the science vs. religion question, from the level of conflicting descriptions of the world to the level of the authority used to justify such views, has a permanent value and message for contemporary discussions about the relations between science and religion. The locus of the debate should not be exclusively, or even primarily, focused on the content differences between the world views involved, but rather on the character of the authority invoked to justify such views. For the first step in solving a problem is to make sure that the problem has been fruitfully formulated.

5. At the authority level, scientific truth is understood to be thoroughly fallibilistic; however that is not the case in regard to truth in religion. This difference in their respective conceptions of truth makes reconciliation between science and religion considerably more difficult.

In science there are, of course, a very large number of laws and theories which the scientist accepts as established truths. But this is always accompanied by the proviso, usually unspoken, that it is possible that future investigations may reveal an error or inaccuracy, which would require a modification or change in the law or theory. The American scientist and philosopher Charles S. Peirce coined the word "fallibilism" to name this openness to the possibility of being in error. As he put it, no scientific claim is absolutely exact, absolutely universal, or absolutely certain.[31]

The two most commonly cited reasons for fallibilism in science are (1) its extensive use of some patterns of inference which are not completely sound logically, as we have already explained, and (2) the increasing prevalence of statistical laws and probability inferences in science since the end of the nineteenth century. To attach the label of "fallibilism" to science does not mean that any particular scientific law or theory is said to be false. Rather it means that such laws and theories are presently accepted as true, but with the proviso that the possibility of falsehood is not excluded as further knowledge is accumulated.

On the other hand Christian theology, especially in the Catholic tradition, maintains that some fundamental religious beliefs, for example, those which comprise the articles of faith in the Nicene Creed, are beyond the possibility of being in error. The reason given for this is that the religious revelation has its source in a God of infallible truth, and this characteristic of truth has been preserved as the revelation has been handed down over the centuries in written and oral religious traditions. As a result religious beliefs which are said to be infallible are said to be true in the especially strong sense that the possibility of error is excluded.

The net result of this is that the mind-set of science and that of religion differ fundamentally on the intrinsic characteristics of truth, and not just on the standards to be used to authorize truth. This in turn causes considerable difficulties for mutual understanding and communication between science and religion.[32] For the mind-set of fallibilism is not congenial to infallibilism, and vice-versa.

This can be easily seen in the thought experiment of simply transposing the truth characteristics of science and religion on this point. The notion that "science is infallible" would be rejected by a scientist as inconsistent with science's epistemic justification through empirical evidence and its rational interpretation. On the other hand the notion of a "fallibilistic Christianity" would be rejected by a theologian, especially in the Catholic tradition, as an unacceptable weakening of the divine origin of revelation and of the Church's authority. It is on this issue of fallibilism vs. infallibilism that one finds the most pronounced divergence between science and religion at the level of their epistemic authority.

Concluding Remarks

We are finally in a position to answer the questions with which we began this lecture. Why are disputes between science and religion so persistent, why are they apparently irresolvable, and why do they serve so easily as occasions for emotional reactions?

The Galileo affair is the classic case of these characteristics. His trial took place in 1633, but it still has not really ended. He himself never was able to find a decisive scientific proof of Copernicanism. But within a few generations after his death, heliocentric astronomy received its full theoretical justification in Newton's laws of gravitation, and its decisive empirical proof in the observation of stellar aberration in 1728 and of stellar parallax in 1838. The scientific issue was definitively settled at that point.

And as long ago as the 1820's the Catholic Church agreed, in effect, that Galileo's scientific views were correct. Yet this dispute continues on up into our own day,[33] which has seen a special effort by Pope John-Paul II in the past few years to put a final end to the Galileo affair. This is not a case of beating a dead horse, because this horse is still alive. Why won't this issue die?

The answer is that there are good grounds to be concerned that there could be another Galileo case in the future over some different set of scientific ideas. Although this may sound like a startling thing to say, it follows rather straightforwardly from our main argument in this lecture.

For as we have seen, conflicts between science and religion appear first at the descriptive level as rivalries between different claims about what the world and human reality are. If that were all that is involved, resolving such differences would be a straightforward intellectual exercise of getting the facts correctly interpreted.

But debates over these competing world views soon touch upon more sensitive nerves at the level of the different authorities behind science and religion. Although elements in the world views may change over time, the underlying authorities do not change. As a result the same basic forces of scientific and religious authority, which resulted in the Galileo affair, are still operative today. That is the reason why fascination with this case continues unabated today, and why it is quite possible that tomorrow another clash similar to the Galileo affair may occur again.

That is also why such conflicts appear to be unresolvable. Furthermore the emotions that they awaken are due to the fact that at the authority level volitional as well as rational factors are involved. For when basic personal commitments are challenged, whether it be in science or in religion, human feelings are unavoidably aroused. In short, it is the interaction between scientific and religious authorities that is at the center of the clashes and debates between science and religion.

Now if any one lesson is to be learned from the Galileo affair, it is that religious authority has its limits. And, of course, scientific authority also has its limits. These two types of authority are not in-

trinsically inconsistent or mutually opposed. So the
old ideal of the unity of all truth remains in place.

The problems arise rather from the misuse of
an authority by extending it into an area beyond its
scope. That is what happened in the Galileo case:
religious authority was used in a misguided attempt
to establish a truth beyond its realm in science.

The opposite, of course, also can and does occur: namely, the misuse of scientific authority to
determine what is true in the realm of religion. An
example of this is Julian Huxley's naturalistic expla-
nation of the Trinity in which God the Father is a
symbol for matter, God the Spirit a symbol for mind,
and God the Son is the symbolic mediation between
mind and matter.[34] Is this "scientific" in any accept-
able sense of the term, or is it not rather a misuse of
scientific authority in the realm of religion? Religious complaints in this type of case are really not
different in kind from science's complaints about
the Galileo affair.

There is, of course, no substitute for good judgment on both sides of the science-religion divide,
and no substitute for respecting the legitimacy and
the value of the epistemic authority behind science
and religion. In the past, such efforts have primarily
taken the form of drawing lines of demarcation *between* the subject matters of science and religion.
But this has not been adequate to the task. For this
borderline is ambiguous since science and religion
overlap, as we have seen, on some very important
topics.

In this common area of serious potential conflicts, what is called for is (1) a better understanding

of the specific characteristics of religious authority and of scientific authority, and (2) a new line of demarcation *within* each authority area which will separate the abuses from the proper uses of these authorities. Any authority, of course, can be abused. But there must be standards which can be employed to identify, and hopefully to avoid, such abuses.

This, of course, is much easier said than done. But without this it is not possible, in our opinion, to improve on the present situation. We make no claims here to having established such standards to judge and avoid abuses of authority. But we do hope that we have succeeded in taking at least the first steps of (1) relocating the central science-religion debate from the descriptive level to the authority level, and (2) of formulating some of the specific characteristics of scientific and religious authority.

There are no reasons to expect that either science or religion will disappear in the foreseeable future, even though there may be a few in each camp who hope for the demise of the other. The explanatory power of science, and the material benefit to human life from the technology which is based upon it, are simply too great to do without them, now that they have been established.

And one must also keep in mind that the ultimate promise of religion is not located primarily at the cognitive level of faith, where potential conflict with science occurs, but in a life of love for others, and in a hope for a transcendent human attainment which has no analogue in science. Religious hope, that often neglected theological virtue, is a call to a greater life. This is the essence of religion, and it has always survived in some form or other in human history. Included in that hope is the confidence that some day the Galileo affair will finally come to an end.

Notes

[1] When we speak throughout this lecture about the relation of religion to science, we are referring only to Christianity, which is characteristically based on a set of revelations contained in its sacred books. Of course, the Judaic and Islamic traditions also are based on such written sources, but for complex reasons they have interacted with science in ways which, although similar, are quite different, and thus they have a different history which is beyond our present discussions. On the other hand, religious traditions which are not based on such revealed sources (for example, religions based on appeals to personal moral or religious experiences), relate to science in still other ways which are also not under consideration in this lecture.

[2] For a development of this point, see A. N. Whitehead, *Science and the Modern World* (New York: Macmillan, 1925) Chapter 1, "The Origins of Modern Science."

[3] This notion was first introduced by Descartes in his *Principia philosophiae*, II, 36 ff.

[4] St. Augustine, *The Literal Meaning of Genesis.* Translated and annotated by John H. Taylor, S. J. (New York: Newman Press, 1982) II, 9, p. 59.

[5] This remark is quoted by Galileo in his *Letter to the Grand Duchess Christina* (1615). See Maurice A. Finocchiaro, ed., *The Galileo Affair: A Documentary History* (Berkeley: University of California Press, 1989) p. 96.

[6] St. Augustine, *The Literal Meaning of Genesis,* I, 19, pp. 42-3.

[7] It is not our purpose here to present a full account of Augustine's exegetical principles, which also include, in addition to what we mention in our text, the notions that the same biblical passage may have multiple meanings, thus counseling prudence in evaluation, and that the language of Scripture is accommodated to the understanding of the common person. For an excellent and fuller discussion of Augustine's exegetical principles as they relate to science, see Ernan McMullin, "Galileo on Science and Scripture," in *The Cambridge Companion to Galileo,* ed. by Peter Machamer (Cambridge University Press - forthcoming).

[8] Thomas Campanella, O. P., *A Defense of Galileo, the Mathematician from Florence.* Translated with an Introduction and Notes by R. J. Blackwell (Notre Dame, IN: University of Notre Dame Press, 1994) pp. 54, 68-69. The reader is referred to the Introduction of this book for an account of Campanella's singular role, and extraordinary personal courage, in the Galileo affair. Early in 1616 Campanella was asked by Cardinal Boniface Caetani, a member of the Sacred Congregation of the Holy Office then examining the orthodoxy of Copernicanism, to submit his theological judgment on the matter to the Holy Office. This request was itself very unusual because at this time Campanella was in the middle of what turned out to be thirty years of a cruel confinement in the prisons of the Inquisition in Naples for his own unorthodox theological views and for his role in actively opposing Spanish hegemony in the Kingdom of Naples. He worked virtually without any source books, relying primarily on his prodigious photographic memory of his earlier reading. His resulting *A Defense of Galileo* is a plea to the Catholic Church to be open to intellectual freedom in general, not because he had any personal or scientific sympathy with Galileo, but because the wel-

fare of the Church itself requires it. Despite his ill-treatment, he remained a loyal member of the Church and of his religious order to the end of his life.

[9] Galileo's letter to Kepler (4 August 1597). Galileo Galilei, *Le Opere di Galileo Galilei*. Edizione Nazionale, cura et labore A. Favaro. 20 vols. (Florence: G. Barbera, 1890-1909. Reprinted: 1929-39; 1964-66) vol. X, p. 68. For an English translation of the relevant passage, see Stillman Drake, *Galileo at Work: His Scientific Biography* (Chicago: University of Chicago Press, 1978) p. 41.

[10] One of the many ironies in the Galileo story is that Copernicus' reworking of astronomy was originally due to a request by the Catholic Church. By the early sixteenth century it had become evident that the Julian calendar, so named because it was introduced by Julius Caesar, was inaccurate by about ten days. Since the date of Easter is determined as the first Sunday after the first full moon after the vernal equinox, the Church needed guidance for the correct dates of religious holy days. Pope Leo X asked Copernicus in 1514 to undertake the needed reform of the calendar. His work on this problem led Copernicus in time to rethink the older geocentric astronomy in order to be able to determine the exact measurement of the length of the solar year. The Gregorian calendar reform, based in part on Copernicus' work, was introduced in 1582 by Pope Gregory XIII, but was only gradually accepted world wide because of the religious strife in Europe after the Reformation. The Julian calendar was reformed by dropping ten days (October 5-14) from the year 1582, and to avoid a later recurrence of the same error, by dropping three leap days (February 29) every 400 years in the century years not evenly divisible by 400. For an excellent set of studies on the Gregorian calendar reform and its delayed acceptance,

see George V. Coyne, S.J., M. A. Hoskin, and O. Pedersen, eds., *Gregorian Reform of the Calendar: Proceedings of the Vatican Conference to Commemorate its 400th Anniversary, 1582-1982* (Vatican City: Pontificia Academia Scientiarum, Specola Vaticana, 1983).

[11] For an account of these developments see Galileo Galilei, *Sidereus Nuncius, or the Sidereal Messenger.* Translated with introduction, conclusion, and notes by Albert van Helden (Chicago: University of Chicago Press, 1989).

[12] For a listing of the most common biblical passages quoted in this debate, see the index in R. J. Blackwell, *Galileo, Bellarmine, and the Bible* (South Bend, IN: University of Notre Dame Press, 1991) pp. 287-88.

[13] Joshua 10: 12-14.

[14] See R. J. Blackwell, *Galileo, Bellarmine, and the Bible,* pp. 5-22, for a discussion of the impact of the Fourth Session of the Council of Trent on the Galileo affair. The quoted part of the decree is taken from pp. 11-12.

[15] For an analysis of Galileo's principles of exegesis, see R. J. Blackwell, *Galileo, Bellarmine, and the Bible,* pp. 64-85, and Ernan McMullin, "Galileo on Science and Scripture," in *The Cambridge Companion to Galileo* (forthcoming from Cambridge University Press).

[16] This of course was not a scientific issue, but a strictly theological debate. Bellarmine advised Paul V in this instance to declare a moratorium on this controversy while the Pope would take the matter under advisement. The Pope accepted this advice, but never did speak later to this issue. Paul V and Bellarmine were the same major figures who had to deal with the Copernicanism vs. the

Bible dispute eight years later, but unfortunately they did not declare a moratorium in that case. For a discussion of this matter see R. J. Blackwell, *Galileo, Bellarmine, and the Bible*, pp. 48-51.

[17] For a full English translation of this treatise, see R. J. Blackwell, *Galileo, Bellarmine, and the Bible*, Appendix VI, pp. 217-52.

[18] This is Bellarmine's letter to Foscarini (12 April 1615), which has been widely reprinted. See M. Finocchiaro, ed., *The Galileo Affair*, pp. 67-69. For additional documents relating to Foscarini's book and Bellarmine's reply, see R. J. Blackwell, *Galileo, Bellarmine, and the Bible*, pp. 253-73.

[19] In his private notes on Bellarmine's letter, Galileo acidly commented that, on this view of "matters of faith and morals," he would be required for eternal salvation to believe that Tobias' unnamed dog in the book of Tobit actually existed, an example chosen obviously because of its trivial status. See R. J. Blackwell, *Galileo, Bellarmine, and the Bible*, pp. 108-09, 269-70.

[20] These corrections were published four years later (15 May 1620), and were relatively minor in character. Book I, Chapter 8 of the *De revolutionibus* was to be dropped, and a few other explicitly realistic statements about heliocentrism were changed or dropped. For these corrections, see M. Finocchiaro, ed., *The Galileo Affair*, pp. 200-02. On the other hand Foscarini's book, which explicitly engaged in scriptural reinterpretation, was condemned without any hope of saving modifications.

[21] For the full text of this critically important decree, see M. Finocchiaro, ed., *The Galileo Affair*, pp. 148-50.

[22] This quotation is from Pope John Paul II's French language address to the Pontifical Academy of Sciences (31 October 1992). The Vatican's English translation of that address can be found in *Origins* (12 November 1992) pp. 370-74. The sentence quoted is from p. 373.

[23] For the full text of the document in the files of the Holy Office, and for the text of Bellarmine's letter to Galileo (26 May 1616), see M. Finocchiaro, ed., *The Galileo Affair,* pp. 147-48, and 153.

[24] These documents are conveniently available in M. Finocchiaro, ed., *The Galileo Affair,* pp. 256-93.

[25] M. Finocchiaro, ed., *The Galileo Affair,* p. 291. The entire text of the sentence is found on pp. 287-91.

[26] Ugo Baldini and George V. Coyne, S. J., *The Louvain Lectures (Lectiones Lovanienses) of Bellarmine and the Autograph Copy of his 1616 Declaration to Galileo* (Vatican City: Specola Vaticana, 1984).

[27] For an excellent discussion of this issue, see Ernan McMullin, *The Inference that Makes Science.* The Aquinas Lecture, 1992 (Milwaukee: Marquette University Press, 1992). Especially Part Four.

[28] Karl R. Popper, *The Logic of Scientific Discovery* (New York: Basic Books, 1959), *Conjectures and Refutations: The Growth of Scientific Knowledge* (New York: Basic Books, 1962), and *Objective Knowledge: An Evolutionary Approach* (Oxford: Clarendon Press, 1972).

[29] Thomas S. Kuhn, *The Structure of Scientific Revolutions* (Chicago: University of Chicago Press, 1962), second edition, enlarged, 1970. For a much fuller and more

recent presentation of Kuhn's views, which has been explicitly endorsed by Kuhn, see Paul Hoyningen-Huene, *Reconstructing Scientific Revolutions: Thomas S. Kuhn's Philosophy of Science.* Translated by Alexander T. Levine (Chicago: University of Chicago Press, 1993).

[30] This notion of religious faith can be found in Thomas Aquinas, *Summa Theologiae,* II-II, 2.

[31] Charles S. Peirce, *Collected Papers of Charles Sanders Peirce.* 6 vols. Edited by Charles Hartshorne and Paul Weiss (Cambridge, MA: Harvard University Press, 1931-35) 1.135-49.

[32] One example of this is that the long-standing Augustinian principle of exegesis (i.e., that in a case of conflict one should accept the teachings of science over a literal reading of Scripture, *if the scientific teaching is conclusively proven*) is no longer usable. For if scientific laws are fallible, they never meet this condition of conclusive proof. When then should the exegete defer to science? "Never" is too strong. But then what degree of probable truth is enough to justify such an interpretation? For example, is evolutionary theory now sufficiently probable to reinterpret Genesis accordingly? More generally, what "modified Augustinian rule" should be employed in such cases?

[33] For a very helpful account of the further history of the Galileo affair after Galileo's death, see Annibale Fantoli, *Galileo: For Copernicanism and for the Church.* Chapter 7.

[34] Julian Huxley, *Religion without Revelation* (New York: Harper & Row, 1957) chapter 2.

THE AQUINAS LECTURES
Published by the Marquette University Press
Milwaukee WI 53201-1881 USA
*Volumes marked * are avaiable as e-books. See web page.*

1. *St. Thomas and the Life of Learning.* John F. McCormick, S.J.
   (1937)   0-87462-101-1

2. *St. Thomas and the Gentiles.* MORTIMER J. ADLER (1938)
                                             0-87462-102-X

3. *St. Thomas and the Greeks.* ANTON C. PEGIS (1939)
                                             0-87462-103-8

4. *The Nature and Functions of Authority.* YVES SIMON (1940)
                                             0-87462-104-6

5. *St. Thomas and Analogy.* GERALD B. PHELAN (1941)
                                             0-87462-105-4

6. *St. Thomas and the Problem of Evil.* JACQUES MARITAIN (1942)
                                             0-87462-106-2

7. *Humanism and Theology.* WERNER JAEGER (1943)
                                             0-87462-107-0

8. *The Nature and Origins of Scientism.* JOHN WELLMUTH (1944)
                                             0-87462-108-9

9. *Cicero in the Courtroom of St. Thomas Aquinas.* E.K. RAND
   (1945)   0-87462-109-7

10. *St. Thomas and Epistemology.* LOUIS-MARIE REGIS, O.P.
    (1946)   0-87462-110-0

11. *St. Thomas and the Greek Moralists.* VERNON J. BOURKE (1947)
                                             0-87462-111-9

About the Aquinas Lecture Series

The Annual St. Thomas Aquinas Lecture Series began at Marquette University in the Spring of 1937. Ideal for classroom use, library additions, or private collections, the Aquinas Lecture Series has received international acceptance by scholars, universities, and libraries. Hardbound in maroon cloth with gold stamped covers. Uniform style and price ($15 each). Some reprints with soft covers. Complete set (60 Titles) (ISBN 0-87462-150-X) receives a 40% discount. New standing orders receive a 30% discount. Regular reprinting keeps all volumes available. Ordering information (purchase orders, checks, and major credit cards accepted):

Book Masters Distribution Services
1444 U.S. Route 42
Ashland OH 44805
Order Toll-Free (800) 247-6553
FAX: (419) 281 6883

Editorial Address:
Dr. Andrew Tallon, Director
Marquette University Press
Box 1881
Milwaukee WI 53201-1881
Tel: (414) 288-7298 FAX: (414) 288-3300
Internet: andrew.tallon@marquette.edu. CompuServe: 73627,1125
Web: http://www.marquette.edu/mupress/

ISBN 0-87462-165-8